SHARK ZONE

BULL SHARK

by Jody Sullivan Rake

Reading Consultant:
Barbara J. Fox
Reading Specialist
North Carolina State University

Content Consultant:
Deborah Nuzzolo
Education Manager
SeaWorld, San Diego

CAPSTONE PRESS
a capstone imprint

Blazers is published by Capstone Press,
151 Good Counsel Drive, P.O. Box 669, Mankato, Minnesota 56002.
www.capstonepub.com

 Books published by Capstone Press are manufactured with paper
containing at least 10 percent post-consumer waste.

Library of Congress Cataloging-in-Publication Data
Rake, Jody Sullivan.
  Bull shark / by Jody Sullivan Rake.
    p. cm.—(Blazers. Shark zone)
  Includes bibliographical references and index.
  Summary: "Describes the bull shark, including physical features, habitat, hunting, and role
in the ecosystem"—Provided by publisher.
  ISBN 978-1-4296-5015-1 (library binding)
  1. Bull shark—Juvenile literature. I. Title. Series.

QL638.95.C3R35 2011
597.3'4—dc22

                                        2010002272

Editorial Credits
Lori Shores, editor; Juliette Peters, designer; Kelly Garvin, media researcher;
    Laura Manthe, production specialist

Photo Credits
Alamy/Michael Patrick O'Neill, 25
Photoshot Holdings/Adrian Hepworth, 7
Seapics/C & M Fallows, 10-11, 20-21; David B. Fleetham, 22-23; David Kearnes, 5, 12,
    16-17; Doug Perrine, cover, 28-29; Mark Conlin, 14-15, 19; Phillip Colla, 9
Shutterstock/artida; Eky Chan; Giuseppe_R, design elements
Tom Stack & Associates, Inc./Andy Murch, 27

Essential content terms are **bold** and are defined on the spread where they first appear.

TABLE OF CONTENTS

CHAPTER 1

UNINVITED GUEST

A huge, football-shaped shark suddenly appears in the **murky** water. It makes quick, sharp turns with its long fins. It bumps fish and turtles with its short nose.

murky—dark or dim due to dirt or other matter

Most sharks find all of their meals in the ocean. But this shark is not in the ocean. This bull shark is hunting in a **freshwater** river.

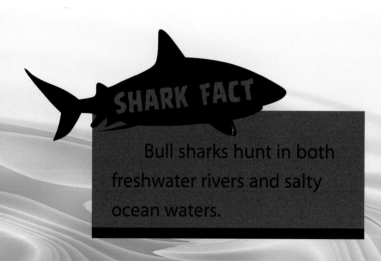

SHARK FACT

Bull sharks hunt in both freshwater rivers and salty ocean waters.

freshwater—water that has little or no salt

CHAPTER 2

TOUGH AND FEARLESS

Bull sharks have chunky bodies. They are 7 to 9 feet (2.1 to 2.7 meters) long. They usually weigh from 200 to 300 pounds (91 to 136 kilograms). The largest bull sharks weigh up to 500 pounds (227 kilograms).

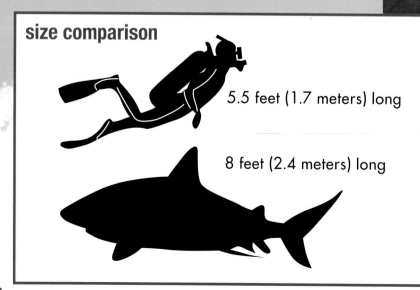

size comparison

5.5 feet (1.7 meters) long

8 feet (2.4 meters) long

SHARK FACT

Bull sharks are one of only
six kinds of sharks that swim in
freshwater rivers.

The bull shark's tail fin pushes it through the water. **Pectoral fins** help it make quick turns. Bull sharks can move easily through tight spaces in narrow rivers.

tail fin

pectoral fin—the hard, flat body part on either side of a shark

pectoral fins

Bull sharks are not picky eaters. They eat almost anything they can find. They hunt mainly fish, but also eat crabs, sea turtles, and stingrays.

SHARK FACT

Animals that come to rivers for water are also meals for bull sharks. Bull sharks have eaten rats, dogs, cows, and antelope!

Bull sharks have small eyes and poor eyesight. Hunting in murky waters makes it even harder for them to see. They depend on their sense of smell to find **prey**.

—an animal hunted by another animal

Bull sharks are **aggressive** and fearless hunters. They will attack prey bigger than themselves. Bull sharks also headbutt prey before they bite it. Bumping prey helps the sharks feel what they can't see.

SHARK FACT

Headbutting and a tough attitude earned the bull shark its name.

aggressive—strong and forceful

CHAPTER 3

GETTING AROUND

Bull sharks live in warm areas around the world. They are usually found in shallow coastal waters and sheltered bays.

Bull Sharks Range

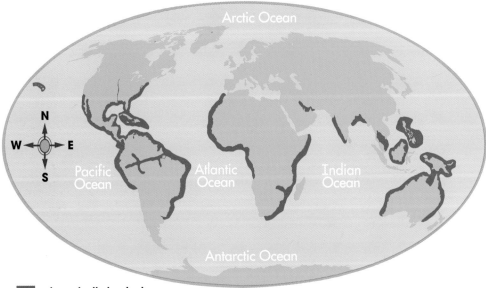

Arctic Ocean

N
W — E
S

Pacific Ocean

Atlantic Ocean

Indian Ocean

Antarctic Ocean

where bull sharks live

Bull sharks move easily between the saltwater ocean and freshwater bays and rivers. They swim up rivers such as the Amazon and the Mississippi. Some bull sharks swim hundreds of miles upstream.

SHARK FACT

Bull sharks in the Caribbean Sea swim up Nicaragua's San Juan River to Lake Nicaragua. The trip is 118 miles (190 kilometers) long.

Bull sharks are an important part of the **ecosystem**. By hunting in rivers, these sharks compete less with sharks that hunt in the ocean. And like other sharks, they help to control fish populations.

ecosystem—a group of animals and plants that work together with their surroundings

CHAPTER 4

A BULLY?

Bull sharks are one of the top three most dangerous sharks. They have attacked people swimming in rivers and seas. Bull shark attacks are reported worldwide.

SHARK FACT

A bull shark once attacked a racehorse swimming in Australia's Brisbane River.

Humans are a **threat** to bull sharks. People catch bull sharks for their meat and tough skins. People also catch fish that bull sharks hunt. These sharks then have less to eat.

SHARK FACT

In Asia, people use bull shark fins in soup.

threat—a person or thing that is seen as a danger

Bull sharks are not **endangered**, but their numbers are decreasing. Bull sharks are not as well known as other sharks. But they are just as important to a healthy ocean.

endangered—at risk of dying out

Glossary

aggressive (uh-GREH-siv)—strong and forceful

ecosystem (EE-koh-sis-tuhm)—a group of animals and plants that work together with their surroundings

endangered (in-DAYN-jurd)—at risk of dying out

freshwater (FRESH-wah-tuhr)—water that has little or no salt; most ponds, rivers, lakes, and streams have freshwater

murky (MUR-kee)—dark or dim due to dirt or other matter

pectoral fin (PEK-tor-uhl FIN)—the hard, flat body part on either side of a shark

prey (PRAY)—an animal hunted by another animal for food

threat (THRET)—a person or thing that is seen as a danger

Read More

Goldish, Meish. *Shark: The Shredder.* Afraid of the Water. New York: Bearport Publishing, 2010.

Randolph, Joanne. *The Great White Shark: King of the Ocean.* Sharks: Hunters of the Deep. New York: PowerKids Press, 2007.

Riehecky, Janet. *Great White Sharks: On the Hunt.* Killer Animals. Mankato, Minn.: Capstone Press, 2009.

Smith, Miranda. *Sharks.* Kingfisher Knowledge. New York: Kingfisher, 2008.

Internet Sites

FactHound offers a safe, fun way to find Internet sites related to this book. All of the sites on FactHound have been researched by our staff.

Here's all you do:

Visit *www.facthound.com*

FactHound will fetch the best sites for you!

Index